PIRATES

PIRATE TREASURE

KENNY ABDO

Fly!
An Imprint of Abdo Zoom
abdobooks.com

abdobooks.com

Published by Abdo Zoom, a division of ABDO, P.O. Box 398166, Minneapolis, Minnesota 55439.

Printed in the United States of America, North Mankato, Minnesota.
102021
012022

THIS BOOK CONTAINS RECYCLED MATERIALS

Photo Credits: Alamy, Granger Collection, iStock, Shutterstock, ©DrStew82 p.16 / CC BY-SA 4.0, ©Svein-Magne Tunli p.18 / CC BY-SA 4.0, ©Theodore Scott p.21 / CC BY 2.0
Production Contributors: Kenny Abdo, Jennie Forsberg, Grace Hansen
Design Contributors: Candice Keimig, Neil Klinepier, Laura Graphenteen

Library of Congress Control Number: 2021940191

Publisher's Cataloging-in-Publication Data

Names: Abdo, Kenny, author.
Title: Pirate treasure / by Kenny Abdo.
Description: Minneapolis, Minnesota : Abdo Zoom, 2022 | Series: Pirates | Includes online resources and index.
Identifiers: ISBN 9781098226886 (lib. bdg.) | ISBN 9781644947036 (pbk.) | ISBN 9781098227722 (ebook) | ISBN 9781098228149 (Read-to-Me ebook)
Subjects: LCSH: Pirates--Juvenile literature. | Treasure troves--Juvenile literature. | Buried treasure--Juvenile literature. | Pirates--History--Juvenile literature. | Piracy--Juvenile literature.
Classification: DDC 910.4--dc23

TABLE OF CONTENTS

PIRATE TREASURE

Pirate lore is full of tales with hidden treasures and maps where “X” marked the spot.

From sunken ships to buried trunks, there are still treasures that continue to **evade** the most seasoned hunters.

YE OLDE YARN

Buried treasure is a collection of stolen objects that is meant to be picked up later. Usually, the treasure is hidden in remote places like islands. Sometimes pirates made maps to help them find the treasure later.

Pirate treasure didn't always include gold or silver. Most of it was food, lumber, cloth, or animal **hides**.

Some pirates didn't bury their treasure right away. They wanted to share the **loot** with their **mates** beforehand.

VAST BOUNTY

Blackbeard said he hid his massive treasure. He just never said where. Hunters have searched for it ever since, looking everywhere from the Caribbean to Virginia, and the Cayman Islands.

The São Vicente was attacked by two pirate ships in 1357 CE. The treasure onboard included gold, silver, and jewels. What happened to the ship and its treasure is still unknown.

In 1699, Captain William Kidd buried millions of dollars in gold and jewels on a small island near New Jersey. He was soon arrested, never able to reclaim his **bounty**. It has yet to be found.

Machiasport, Maine, is possibly home to a treasure worth millions of dollars. Samuel Bellamy dropped anchor there before he was captured for his crimes. Bellamy never made his way back to the riches he left behind.

Captain Thomas Cavendish buried some of his riches at Palemano Point in Hawaii. Explorers have tried to locate the treasures and the wreckage of the captain's ship. So far, nothing has been found.

Treasure worth more than $100 million may be buried on **Seychelles** in the Indian Ocean. Pirate Olivier Levasseur took over a ship not knowing what was on it.

Levasseur disappeared and is believed to have hidden his treasure on the island country.

The Treasure of Lima was a haul of Spanish gold, silver, and jewels. Stolen by Captain William Thompson, he buried the **loot** on Costa Rica's Cocos Islands. Treasure hunters have yet to find it.

Stolen treasures like food, wood, and cloth were rarely buried. But for those looking for riches, "X" marks the spot. And hunters will also be digging up history with their fortunes!

GLOSSARY

bounty – a large sum of money or treasure gained or won.

evade – to escape or avoid.

hide – animal skin and fur treated for human use like coats and blankets.

loot – goods or private property taken from someone else.

mate – a fellow member of a ship's crew.

Seychelles – an island country made up of a group of islands located on the Indian Ocean off the east coast of Africa.

ONLINE RESOURCES

Booklinks
NONFICTION NETWORK
FREE! ONLINE NONFICTION RESOURCES

To learn more about Pirate Treasure, please visit **abdobooklinks.com** or scan this QR code. These links are routinely monitored and updated to provide the most current information available.

INDEX